# Content

The first whales............... 2
Keeping warm................ 4
How whales breathe.......... 6
Swimming, diving and leaping..... 8
Whale song.................. 12
Baby whales................. 14
The Blue whale.............. 16
The Killer whale............. 18
How whales live............. 20
How long whales live......... 22
Glossary.................... 24

# The first whales

Did you know that the first whales had legs and could walk? They could walk on the land.

*This whale could walk on the land.*

Now whales are animals that live in the sea. They live in the sea all the time. They cannot live on the land at all. They don't have any legs at all.

*Now whales live in the sea.*

# Keeping warm

A whale is an animal with warm blood, like us. This means that it has to keep its blood warm all the time. It has fat under its skin to keep its blood warm.

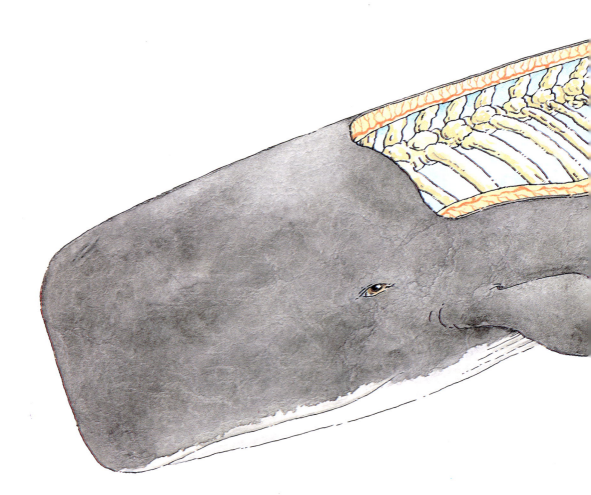

The fat under a whale's skin is very thick. It can be sixty centimetres thick. This thick fat is called blubber.

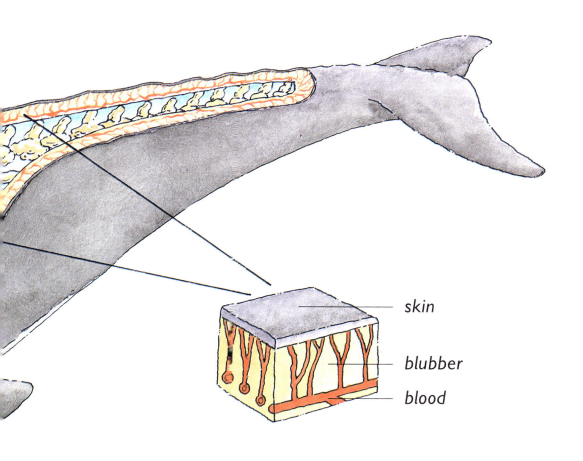

Blubber keeps the whale's blood warm.

# How whales breathe

Whales breathe the air, like us. This means that they cannot breathe under the sea. They have to come up to breathe the air.

*Whales come up from the sea to breathe the air.*

Whales have a blowhole on the top of their heads. They use the blowhole to breathe in air. They also use the blowhole to blow air out again.

This whale is breathing out.

# Swimming, diving and leaping

Whales have a smooth shape. Their smooth shape helps them to swim. They also have large flippers. The large flippers help them to swim, too.

*These whales are swimming under the sea.*

Whales have a large tail fin. Their large tail fin is called a fluke. The fluke fin helps the whale to swim.

*The large tail fin is called a fluke.*

Whales can dive very well. They can dive very fast and very deep. Their smooth shape helps them to dive fast and deep.

*This whale is diving.*

Some whales like to leap. This whale can leap right out of the sea. When whales leap right out of the sea, it is called breaching.

*This whale is breaching.*

# Whale song

Whales do not have ears like us, but they can hear. They can also make a loud sound. The loud sound that they make is called whale song.

*Whales make a sound called whale song.*

The whale song helps the whale to find food. The whale song echoes under the sea. The whale can tell from the echoes where there is food.

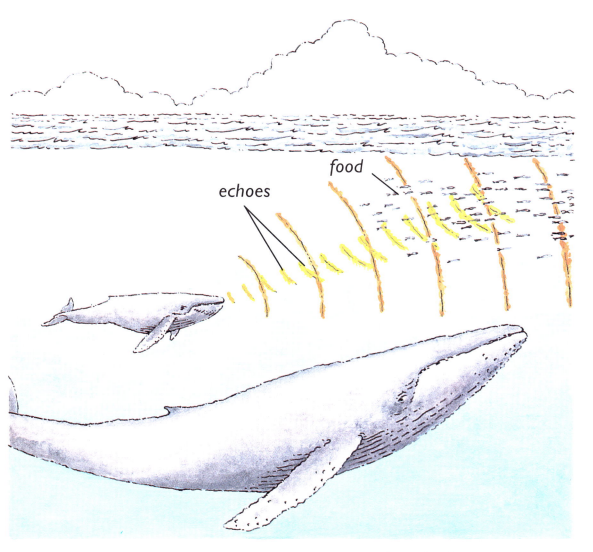

Whale song helps the whale to find food.

# Baby whales

Whales can have baby whales. They only have one baby at a time. A baby whale is called a calf.

*This whale has a whale calf with it.*

Whale calves are very heavy. No other baby animals are as heavy as whale calves. Just one whale calf can be as heavy as three small cars!

A whale calf can be as heavy as three small cars.

# The Blue whale

This whale is very large. It is called the Blue whale. It is the largest animal that has ever lived.

*The Blue whale is a very large animal.*

The Blue whale does not have teeth. It has a filter in its mouth. It can filter a lot of food out of the sea.

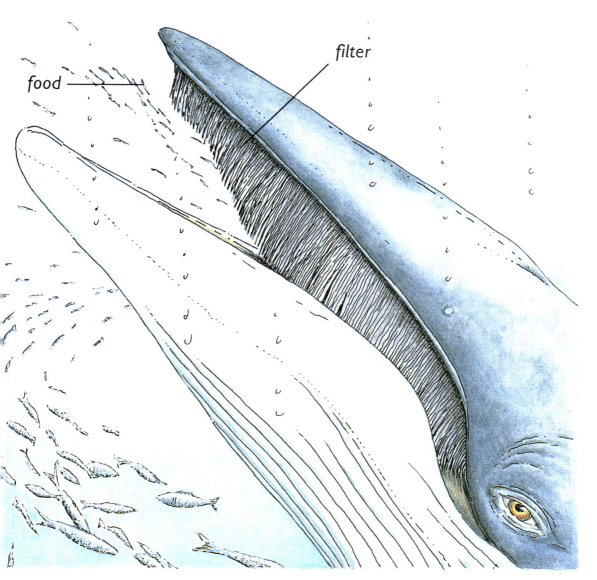

The Blue whale filters food out of the sea.

# The Killer whale

This is the Killer whale. The Killer whale has teeth. Its teeth look like pegs. The Killer whale's teeth help it to catch food.

*The Killer whale's teeth look like pegs.*

The Killer whale likes to catch fish, seals and even penguins. It slides onto the ice to catch the seals and penguins. Then it slides off the ice and into the sea again.

*The Killer whale slides onto the ice to catch a seal.*

## How whales live

The Blue whale likes to live alone. Sometimes it will live with just one other whale. It does not like to live with a lot of whales.

*The Blue whale likes to live alone.*

The Killer whale likes to live in a group. A group of whales is called a pod. How many whales can you see in this pod?

*Killer whales like to live in a group called a pod.*

# How long whales live

Some whales do not live very long. Small whales have a lifespan of about ten years. Bigger whales have a longer lifespan.

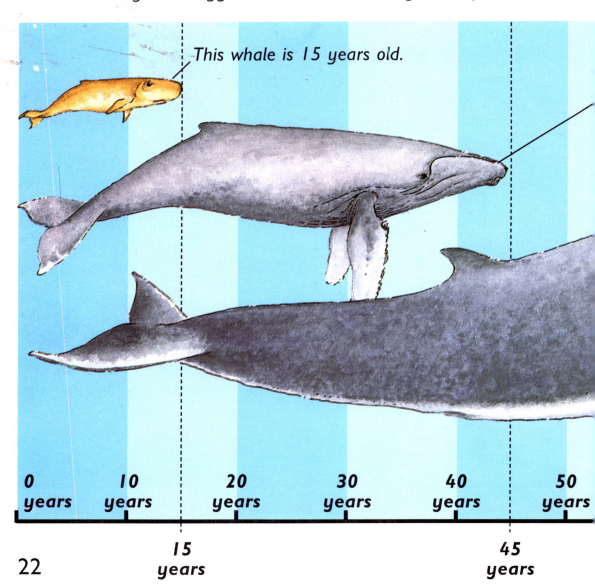

This whale is 15 years old.

0 years | 10 years | 15 years | 20 years | 30 years | 40 years | 45 years | 50 years

Blue whales have the longest lifespan of any whale. The Blue whale can live for about 110 years.

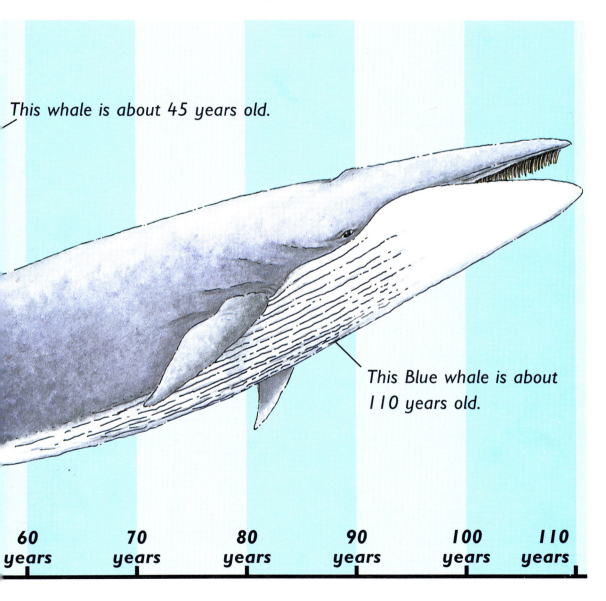

This whale is about 45 years old.

This Blue whale is about 110 years old.

| 60 years | 70 years | 80 years | 90 years | 100 years | 110 years |

 # Glossary

**blowhole**
a whale uses a blowhole to breathe in and out
**blubber**
the thick fat under the whale's skin
**Blue whale**
the largest kind of whale; also the largest animal
**echo**
a sound that comes back to you
**flippers**
parts of a whale that help it to swim
**fluke fin**
a whale's large tail fin
**Killer whale**
a whale that has teeth
**penguin**
a large black and white bird that cannot fly; it lives on the land and in the sea
**pod**
a group of whales
**seal**
an animal that lives on the land and in the sea